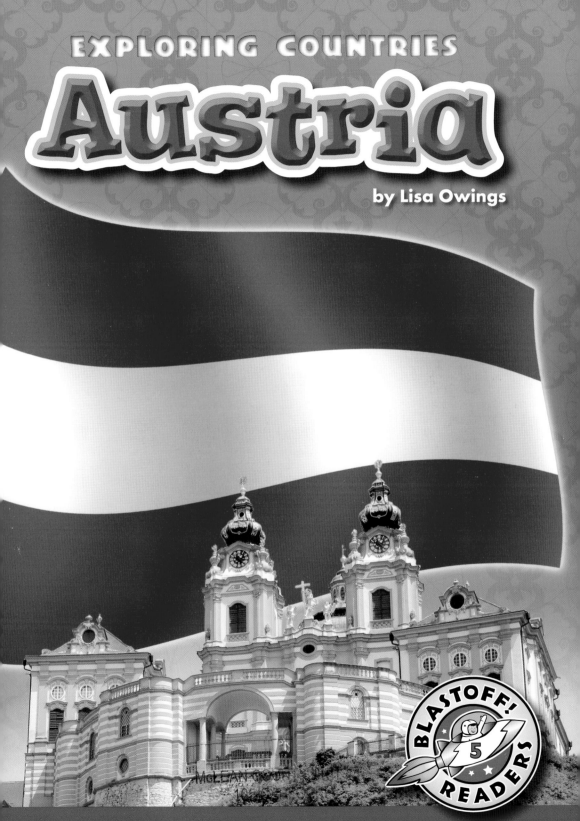

EXPLORING COUNTRIES

Austria

by Lisa Owings

BELLWETHER MEDIA • MINNEAPOLIS, MN

Note to Librarians, Teachers, and Parents:

Blastoff! Readers are carefully developed by literacy experts and combine standards-based content with developmentally appropriate text.

Level 1 provides the most support through repetition of high-frequency words, light text, predictable sentence patterns, and strong visual support.

Level 2 offers early readers a bit more challenge through varied simple sentences, increased text load, and less repetition of high-frequency words.

Level 3 advances early-fluent readers toward fluency through increased text and concept load, less reliance on visuals, longer sentences, and more literary language.

Level 4 builds reading stamina by providing more text per page, increased use of punctuation, greater variation in sentence patterns, and increasingly challenging vocabulary.

Level 5 encourages children to move from "learning to read" to "reading to learn" by providing even more text, varied writing styles, and less familiar topics.

Whichever book is right for your reader, Blastoff! Readers are the perfect books to build confidence and encourage a love of reading that will last a lifetime!

This edition first published in 2015 by Bellwether Media, Inc.

No part of this publication may be reproduced in whole or in part without written permission of the publisher. For information regarding permission, write to Bellwether Media, Inc., Attention: Permissions Department, 5357 Penn Avenue South, Minneapolis, MN 55419.

Library of Congress Cataloging-in-Publication Data

Owings, Lisa.
  Austria / by Lisa Owings.
    pages cm. – (Blastoff! Readers: Exploring Countries)
  Includes bibliographical references and index.
  Summary: "Developed by literacy experts for students in grades three through seven, this book introduces young readers to the geography and culture of Austria"– Provided by publisher.
  ISBN 978-1-60014-983-2 (hardcover : alkaline paper)
  1. Austria–Juvenile literature. I. Title.
  DB17.O95 2014
  943.6–dc23
                                                            2014002723

Printed in the United States of America, North Mankato, MN.

Contents

Where Is Austria?

Germany

Did you know?
The beloved movie *The Sound of Music* was filmed in Salzburg, Austria.

Liechtenstein

Switzerland

Italy

Austria is a small country in the heart of Europe. Its borders surround 32,383 square miles (83,871 square kilometers) of stunning mountains and forests. Vienna is the capital of Austria. The city lies in the northeast along the Danube River.

Austria is surrounded by many other countries. Italy and Slovenia lie directly to the south. To the west are Switzerland and tiny Liechtenstein. Germany and the Czech Republic share long borders with Austria to the north. The country's neighbors to the east are Slovakia and Hungary. No part of Austria reaches the sea.

Alps

Austria's landscape is famed for its beauty. The snowcapped peaks of the Alps stretch from the western border to the center of the country. Forests grow on the mountain slopes. Long ago, **glaciers** carved deep valleys between the mountains. They also left behind cold, clear lakes.

North of the Alps, emerald hills roll toward the Danube River. Most Austrian rivers flow to join the Danube. On the other side of this great river are more wooded hills and mountains. **Lowlands** cover the eastern part of the country. Winters in Austria are cold, especially in the mountains. People living in eastern Austria enjoy warm summers.

fun fact

The Danube is the second longest river in Europe. It flows through nine countries before emptying into the Black Sea.

Did you know?
Austrians have started covering Alpine ski slopes in white cloth during summer. The cloth helps keep the snow from melting.

The Alps began to form around 65 million years ago. Over time, forces inside the earth caused the land in central Europe to lift and crumple. **Erosion** shaped the young mountains into those seen today. The Alps cover nearly two-thirds of Austria. They are frosted by white glaciers and surrounded by blue lakes. Waterfalls rush down their steep slopes.

The Grossglockner is the highest peak in the Austrian Alps. It reaches a towering 12,460 feet (3,798 meters). This mountain also features the country's longest glacier. Grossglockner and several other tall peaks lie within Hohe Tauern National Park. This park is the the largest protected area in Central Europe.

! fun fact

A kind of mountain music called yodeling took shape in the Alps. The high pitches and quick note changes were a way of communicating far across the mountains.

Grossglockner

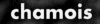

chamois

Austria's mountains and forests shelter many wild animals. The marmot's high-pitched whistle echoes across the Alps. Herds of goat-like chamois spend summers high in the mountains. In winter, they **graze** alongside red deer in lower forests. Ibex also climb the Alpine slopes. Their long horns make them easy to spot.

fox

marmot

golden
eagle

Golden eagles soar above Alpine peaks. Vultures
circle, hoping for leftover meals. Scurrying across the
countryside are foxes and other small animals. Graceful
swans and storks seek out wetlands in the east. The
country's rivers are full of perch, pike, and rainbow trout.

fun fact

Traditional Austrian clothing for men and boys includes *Lederhosen*. These are leather shorts held up by suspenders. Women and girls wear *Dirndls*. These dresses have full skirts and aprons.

Austria is home to more than 8 million people. About nine out of every ten are Austrian. Their **ancestors** were originally from the country. They speak a **dialect** of German, which is Austria's official language.

Many **immigrants** came to Austria in the late 1900s during the **Cold War**. They include people from Bosnia and Herzegovina, Croatia, Serbia, and Slovenia. People from Germany, Hungary, and Turkey also live in the country. Each group speaks their own language in their own community. However, nearly all immigrants also speak German.

Speak German!

English	German	How to say it
hello	servus	SEHR-voos
good-bye	auf wiedersehen	owf VEE- der-zay-en
yes	ja	yah
no	nein	nine
please	bitte	BIT-tuh
thank you	danke	DAHN-kah
friend	freund	froind

Most Austrians live in cities and towns. Families in cities often rent an apartment instead of buying a home. The Austrian government helps people pay for apartments. In the countryside, two-story houses are more common. Austrians love to decorate their homes with bright flowers.

Buses and trains are common ways to travel in large cities. Most Austrians also drive from place to place. Children often walk or bike. Even when running errands, Austrians like to dress nicely. They stroll down streets lined with shops or market stalls. People wear **traditional** Austrian clothes for special occasions. This is one way Austrians show pride in their culture.

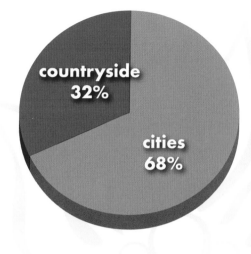

Where People Live in Austria

countryside 32%

cities 68%

All Austrian children go to school from ages 6 to 15. During the first four years, they learn arts and crafts, German, social studies, and math. Then they move on to secondary school. Students choose which type of secondary school to attend.

Around age 14, Austrians begin to focus on a career path. Some take **apprenticeships** until they can enter the workforce. Many continue at secondary schools that teach specific jobs. Other secondary schools offer classes that help prepare students for college. Graduates can apply to one of Austria's universities or fine arts schools.

Where People Work in Austria

manufacturing 26%

farming 5.5%

services 68.5%

About two out of every three Austrians choose to work in **service jobs**. Many work for the government in banks, schools, and hospitals. Others help preserve the nation's culture at museums, theaters, and concert halls. Austria attracts millions of **tourists** each year. Staff at restaurants and resorts help these travelers enjoy their stay.

Some Austrians **harvest** oil, coal, and iron ore from the land. Factory workers turn these items into fuel, iron, and steel. They also make cars, machinery, and chemicals. Mountainous Austria has little farmland. Yet farmers find space to raise cows or grow barley, beets, or apples. Austrian farmers are able to feed most of the country.

Surrounded by snowy peaks, it is no wonder Austrians enjoy winter sports. People of all ages love downhill skiing. Snowboarding, ice skating, and hockey are other popular sports. Austrians go hiking, mountain climbing, and biking in summer. On hot days, people head to the nearest lake to go swimming or boating. Austrians also gather at stadiums to cheer on their favorite soccer team.

Cultural activities are equally important to Austrians. They enjoy going to operas, plays, and concerts. Many make music of their own with local bands or choirs. For vacations, families often travel around Europe. Austrians also like to share meals with friends at restaurants.

Did you know?

The Lipizzaner horses at the Spanish Riding School in Vienna are an important part of Austrian culture. These pure white horses learn complex movements and jumps to show off at performances.

Did you know?

In the past, most Austrians ate their main meal at midday. Now, it is more common to prepare a large meal in the evening after work.

Austrians love to **indulge** in rich meats and pastries. *Wiener Schnitzel,* a breaded **veal** dish, is famous worldwide. Fried chicken and boiled beef are other popular dishes. Meat is often served with dumplings called *Knödel.* Roadside stands sell sausages to people looking for a quick bite.

Austria is also famous for its sweets. Apple strudel is dusted with sugar and served with coffee. The jam-filled Linzer torte is another favorite. One of the richest Austrian pastries is the Sacher torte. This chocolate creation is a great way to end a meal.

Wiener Schnitzel

apple strudel

Did you know?
Austrian Franz Gruber wrote the music for the Christmas carol "Silent Night, Holy Night" in 1818.

Christmas market

Frohe Weihnachten

Austrian celebrations are full of traditions. The Salzburg Festival is held in summer. People come from all over the world to enjoy fine music and theater performances. On October 26, Austrians celebrate National Day. Many spend the day visiting museums, which open their doors to the public for free on this day.

Throughout December, Austrians prepare for Christmas. They decorate their homes and set up holiday markets in town squares. Most of the festivities take place on December 24. Families gather to sing carols and open presents. In the mountains, Glöcklerlauf is celebrated on January 5. People wearing loud bells and giant headdresses parade through the streets. Their actions are thought to chase away evil winter spirits.

Did you know?

Vienna remains a center for classical music today. Musicians and composers come from all over the world to study in the city.

Wolfgang Amadeus Mozart

Ludwig
van Beethoven

Franz
Schubert

As a musical center of Europe, Vienna has attracted
many of history's most famous **composers**. Joseph
Haydn was born in Austria in 1732. His musical
talent drew the attention of Austrian royals. Haydn
wrote hundreds of pieces for orchestras and smaller
groups. The younger Wolfgang Amadeus Mozart
was a child **prodigy**. He became good friends with
Haydn after moving to Vienna. Also a native Austrian,
Mozart excelled at nearly every musical style.

Ludwig van Beethoven came to Vienna from Germany.
He greatly admired Mozart and studied under Haydn.
Despite his hearing loss, Beethoven changed the
way people felt about music. His pieces often move
audiences to tears. Austrians today are proud to
share their history of great music with the world.

Fast Facts About Austria

Austria's Flag

The flag of Austria has three horizontal bands of red, white, and red. Government flags also have a black eagle in the center. The striped design is said to go back to a fierce battle in 1191. Stories say Duke Leopold V of Austria had been splattered with blood. His white shirt had turned red except for the band under his belt. From then on, the red and white banner was connected with Austria.

Official Name: Republic of Austria

Area: 32,383 square miles (83,871 square kilometers); Austria is the 114th largest country in the world.

Capital City:	Vienna
Important Cities:	Graz, Linz, Salzburg, Innsbruck
Population:	8,221,646 (July 2013)
Official Language:	German
National Holiday:	National Day (October 26)
Religions:	Christian (78.3%), Muslim (4.2%), other (3.5%), unspecified (2%), none (12%)
Major Industries:	services, tourism, manufacturing
Natural Resources:	oil, coal, timber, iron ore, copper, salt, magnesite
Manufactured Products:	metals, machinery, cars, chemicals, clothing, food products
Farm Products:	wheat, corn, barley, sugar beets, potatoes, apples, grapes, cows, pigs
Unit of Money:	Euro; the euro is divided into 100 cents.

Glossary

ancestors—relatives who lived long ago

apprenticeships—positions in which someone who wants to learn a job works under someone who is very good at that job

Cold War—the state of tension between the United States and former Soviet Union from 1945 to 1991

composers—people who write music

dialect—a unique way of speaking a language; dialects are often specific to certain regions of a country.

erosion—the slow wearing away of soil and rock by water or wind

glaciers—massive sheets of ice that cover large areas of land

graze—to feed on grasses and plants

harvest—to gather

immigrants—people who leave one country to live in another

indulge—to allow oneself to have or do something as a special pleasure

lowlands—areas of land that are lower than the surrounding land

prodigy—a young person who is unusually talented at something

service jobs—jobs that perform tasks for people or businesses

tourists—people who travel to visit another place

traditional—related to a custom, idea, or belief handed down from one generation to the next

veal—the meat of young cattle

To Learn More

AT THE LIBRARY

Carew-Miller, Anna. *Ludwig van Beethoven: Great Composer*. Broomall, Penn.: Mason Crest, 2014.

Grahame, Deborah A. *Austria*. New York, N.Y.: Marshall Cavendish Benchmark, 2007.

Peppas, Lynn. *The Alps*. New York, N.Y.: Crabtree Pub. Co., 2012.

ON THE WEB

Learning more about Austria is as easy as 1, 2, 3.

1. Go to www.factsurfer.com.

2. Enter "Austria" into the search box.

3. Click the "Surf" button and you will see a list of related web sites.

With factsurfer.com, finding more information is just a click away.

Index

The images in this book are reproduced through the courtesy of: JeniFoto, front cover (top), p. 14; Maisei Raman, front cover (bottom), p. 28; John Warburton Lee/ SuperStock, pp. 6-7; Borus Stroujko, p. 7; mbbirdy, p. 8; Max Topchii, p. 9; Raimund Linke/ Corbis Images, pp. 10-11; Menno Schaefer, p. 11 (top); Christian Musat, p. 11 (middle); Andy Dean Photography, p. 11 (bottom); Hans Huber/ Glow Images, p. 12; vvoe, p. 15; Christian Vorhofer/ imagebroker/ age fotostock, pp. 16-17; Cultura Limited/ SuperStock, p. 18; Chromorange/ Bilderbox/ Newscom, p. 19 (left); Bruce Yuanyue Bi/ Getty Images, p. 19 (right); dell640, p. 20; Lilli Strauss/ AP Images, p. 21; Martin Siepmann/ Alamy, p. 22; Valentin Kolesnicov, p. 23 (left); Jerry Sliwowski, p. 23 (right); Burben, pp. 24-25; S. Borisov, p. 26; HultonArchive, p. 27 (left); The Art Archive/ SuperStock, p. 27 (right).